Spending Less and Enjoying It More

Spending Less and Enjoying It More

Harper A. Roehm CPA, DBA

MC GRAW-HILL BOOK COMPANY

New York St. Louis San Francisco Auckland Bogotá Guatemala
Hamburg Johannesburg Lisbon London Madrid Mexico Montreal
New Delhi Panama Paris San Juan São Paulo
Singapore Sydney Tokyo Toronto

1 2 3 4 5 6 7 8 9 0 SEMSEM 8 7 6 5 4

ISBN 0-07-053417-9

Library of Congress Cataloging in Publication Data

Roehm, Harper A.
Spending less and enjoying it more.
1. Home economics--Accounting. I. Title.
TX326.R63 1984 640'.42 83-11334
ISBN 0-07-053417-9

To Sally

CONTENTS

PREFACE

Most of us have a hard time "making it" financially. No matter how much money we make, expenses seem to grow faster than income. The pressures, anxiety, and stress caused by worries over money affect everyone. Many feel that they do not have an adequate income to pay necessary expenses, and others are frustrated by their failure to save. The purpose of this book is to show you that you do have control of your money, that you can manage your spending more effectively, and that, by properly recognizing priorities, you can "Spend Less and Enjoy It More."

The first step in dealing with this situation is to make a start at money management by using a personal budget that really works. This book, devoted solely to personal budgeting, outlines a process that has evolved from my personal budgeting experience over the last twenty years. My success with this process prompted me to share it with others.

Most people are ineffective at budgeting because they do not understand either its behavioral or mechanical aspects. This book discusses how our spending habits reveal our fears and frustrations as well as our preferences, and how successful budgeting depends on our recognizing these patterns and setting spending priorities which include them. It also provides detailed and easy-to-follow instructions with a complete and continuous example. The unique procedure enables us to identify those expenses which we control and allows for adjustments as individual priorities change.

For most people, especially those starting out--new graduates, newly married couples--this book provides a vehicle and a focal point for discovering certain behavioral aspects about themselves. How we spend money is a reflection of our priority structures. Understanding this and learning to identify what is really important to us helps in making meaningful daily decisions.

There are three phases to the budget process. While each phase is dependent on the previous one, it is not necessary to complete each phase to improve the management of our money. Phase 1 requires the preparation of an annual budget and enables us to see where overall expenses can be better controlled. This phase also provides an excellent record and source of information about family finances which otherwise would not be available. This becomes important when a breadwinner dies or a marriage breaks up. Phase 2 distributes Phase-1 data by months and allows us to identify any potential monthly cash flow problem. Finally, Phase 3 provides an easy procedure for managing monthly expenses. The book emphasizes planning and does not require us to record each expense incurred, in order to gain control.

I would like to thank Kathy Kear for help in typing the earlier drafts and Jacqueline McHale for her efforts in preparation of the final drafts. A special note of gratitude is extended to Donna Kinlin for her suggestions and assistance in editing and reviewing. Also, I would like to thank Steve Bailey for his comments.

Chapter 1

The Budget Process

Do you feel overwhelmed by your monthly bills and expenses? Are you concerned about being able to "make it" financially from month to month? Are you afraid that you will never be able to save enough money for a down payment on a house, your children's education, or your retirement? Is your marriage threatened by failure to agree on how to properly manage your finances? The list of common financial fears is long and familiar.

Fifteen years ago, my wife and I made an important decision that required a substantial cut in family income. I left a secure job as an internal auditor in a large corporation to accept a teaching position at half the salary. Of course, we had to make careful decisions about what our spending priorities would be. It was the experience of working through these decisions and coping with an even more drastic income cut several years later that evolved the budgeting process in this manual.

This budget manual will assist you in gaining control of your personal finances. The purpose of budgeting is to motivate your future behavior so that you will not only spend within your financial capability but also maximize your personal goals and enjoyment. To accomplish this, the budget procedure described is very explicit. It also considers the vital aspects of spending behavior, especially the recognition and acceptance of individual differences in spending preferences.

Often, budgeting is viewed as a process where each expense must be recorded and detailed records maintained. When budgeting is approached as a tedious bookkeeping job, the process usually fails. A major advantage of my budget procedure is that it emphasizes planning with no requirement for maintaining detailed expense records.

There are three mechanical phases to this budget process. Although each phase builds on the one preceding it, all three phases need not be completed. Improvements in financial control can be made by adopting only one or two of the techniques included. The first phase requires preparation of an annual budget. The second phase breaks down the annual figures into monthly increments, and the third phase illustrates a method for calculating both the maximum and minimum amounts that can be saved. The next few pages preview the final products of each phase to illustrate how easy, how valuable, and how effective this budgeting process can be. An example of the final product produced from Phase 1--a one-year budget--follows. Please note:

Line 8. Total cash available after all expenses have been paid is short $150.
Line 9. We would like to save $1,200.
Line 10. If we add the $150 to the $1,200, we will need to adjust our budget (reduce expenses) by $1,350.

On the positive side:

Line 6. Our cash receipts exceed our annual fixed, monthly fixed, and monthly operational expenses by $7,044.
Line 7. In other words, we have $7,044 available to pay our discretionary expenses of $7,149. (Discretionary expenses are those which we control. We decide _if_ we are going to incur them and _when_.)

Further, there are adequate cash receipts available to pay for all necessary expenses. Only those expenses which the individual controls must be adjusted.

The detail and quality of Phases 2 and 3 depend on the careful preparation of Phase 1. The end product of Phase 2 is illustrated on the next two pages.

FORM AB-12

BUDGET SUMMARY--ANNUAL

LINE		THIS YEAR	REVISIONS 1	REVISIONS 2
1. Annual Cash Receipts		$ 25,527 (salary, interests, etc.)		
Add:				
2. Annual Fixed Expenses	+	$ 2,355 (taxes, insurance, etc.)		
3. Monthly Fixed Expenses	+	$ 5,328 (house payment, utilities, etc.)		
4. Monthly Operational Expenses	+	$ 10,800 (food, entertainment, etc.)		
5. Total (lines 2, 3, 4)		$ 18,483		
Deduct line 5 from line 1 (Annual Cash Receipts) to get line 6				
6. Cash Available for Discretionary Expenses		$ 7,044		
7. Deduct Discretionary Expenses	-	$ 7,194 (auto repair, clothing,etc.)		
8. Total Cash Available After All Expenses				
Cash Excess				
Cash Short ( )		$ (150)		
9. Deduct Desired Savings		$ (1,200)		
10. Required Adjustment		$ (1,350)		

The second phase ends with a monthly summary. It takes the numbers developed in Phase 1 and allocates them to each month. The next page illustrates the allocation for the first three month's expenses. Please note:

January

Line		Amount
1.	Monthly receipts	$ 2,127
5.	The annual fixed, plus fixed monthly, plus monthly operational expenses are deducted	$-1,719
6.	To obtain the amount available for discretionary expenses (discretionary expenses are those you can control)	$ 408
7.	Discretionary expenses are deducted	$- 635
8.	To obtain a cash shortage of	$ (227)
9.	The cash shortage is added to the beginning balance	-0-
10.	To obtain the cumulative balance of	$ (227)

The first column tells the budget preparer that if he spends all the money he budgets for January, he will be $227 short for the month. However, he has $635 of discretionary expenses (line 7) which he may choose not to incur. Line 6 indicates that he has $408 available to spend towards his discretionary expenses.

Going on to February, line 6 indicates that there is $683 available to pay February's discretionary expenses of $425. After paying all of February's expenses, $258 remain (line 8). The obvious solution to January's problem then is to postpone $227 of January's discretionary expenses and incur them in February.

FORM MB-3

MONTHLY SUMMARY

LINE		JAN	FEB	MAR
1. Annual Cash Receipts		$ 2,127	$ 2,127	$ 2,127
Add:				
2. Annual Fixed Expenses	+	$ 425	$ 150	$ 185
3. Monthly Fixed Expenses	+	$ 444	$ 444	$ 444
4. Monthly Operational Expenses	+	$ 850	$ 850	$ 850
5. Total (lines 2, 3, 4)		$ 1,719	$ 1,444	$ 1,479
Deduct line 5 from line 1 (Annual Cash Receipts) to get line 6				
6. Cash Available for Discretionary Expenses		$ 408	$ 683	$ 648
7. Deduct Discretionary Expenses	-	$ 635	$ 425	$ 150
8. Total Cash Available After All Expenses				
Cash Excess		$	$ 258	$ 498
Cash Short ( )		$ (227)		
9. Add Beginning Balance	+	$ -0-	$ (227)	$ 31
10. Ending Balance	+	$	$ 31	$ 529
Negative ( )		$ (227)		

Phase 3 concludes the process with the preparation of the "Mini/Max Savings Projection." The next page illustrates this schedule. Again, note January.

Line 1 The maximum amount that can be saved is $408 if none of the discretionary expenses are incurred. Remember, discretionary expenses are those you control. You may or may not spend the money. The $408 comes directly from Phase 2 on the monthly schedule, line 6, illustrated on page 5.

Line 2 The minimum amount that can be saved this month is a negative $227 if you decide to incur all of the discretionary expenses. This amount comes directly from Phase 2 on the monthly schedule, line 8, page 5.

This schedule is prepared at the beginning of each year from Phase-2 data. Each month the budget preparer deducts that month's total expenses from total receipts and compares the remaining figure to the mini/max savings projection for that month. For example, let us assume that we list the following cash receipts and expenses for the month of June, which leaves us with $300:

Total Receipts	$1,800
Deduct Total Expenses	$1,500
Total available for saving	$ 300

When we compare the $300 available for savings in June to our projected mini/max schedule, we see that the maximum we should be able to save is $833 and the minimum is $233. Since the $300 falls between the two amounts, we know that we are probably in control of our expenses. On the bottom two lines, we also have the cumulative mini/max amounts that we should have saved since the beginning of the year. By the end of June, we should have saved a minimum of $1,218.

FORM MM-1

MINI/MAX SAVINGS PROJECTION

LINE	JAN	FEB	MAR	APR	MAY	JUN	JUL	AUG	SEP	OCT	NOV	DEC
1. Maximum monthly savings	408	683	648	833	773	833	193	383	663	558	833	836
2. Minimum monthly savings *	(227)	258	498	533	(77)	233	(886)	(408)	213	(167)	622	608
3. Maximum year-to-date savings	408	1091	1739	2572	3345	4178	4371	4754	5417	5975	6808	7644
4. Minimum year-to-date savings	(227)	31	529	1062	985	1218	332	(76)	137	(30)	592	1200

If after deducting monthly expenses from monthly cash receipts you are saving:

1. An amount between the minimum (line 2) and maximum (line 1), and

2. Your accumulative savings for the year fall between minimum (line 4) and maximum (line 3), you are effectively managing your finances and should be achieving your desired financial goals.

*These amounts are the minimum savings necessary each month in order to pay all projected expenses and save $1,200 for the year (line 4, December).

The purpose of this manual is to help you live within your financial means and, at the same time, get more satisfaction from your money. To accomplish this objective, the mechanical process of personal budgeting must be explicit. This manual incorporates three major mechanical phases, with its own procedures and set of forms. They are:

Budget	Time Required: Now	Time Required: In the Future
1. Phase 1--Preparation of Annual Budget 2. Phase 2--Allocation of Annual Budget to a Monthly Budget	2 evenings	All phases Completed in one evening
3. Phase 3--Monthly Management of Actual Expenses	1 evening	

While each phase depends on the preceding phase, it is not necessary to perform each phase. One may only prepare an annual budget (Phase 1) which will give some idea where overall expenses might be cut in order to meet objectives and live within your available income. Another major advantage of preparing an annual budget is that it provides an excellent record and source of information about family revenues and expenses which otherwise may not be available. This becomes extremely important when a breadwinner dies or a marriage breaks up. Finally, people who are "starting out"--new graduates or newly married couples--can avoid the undue pressure caused from failing to properly manage their finances.

The second phase--allocation of the annual budget to a monthly budget--provides additional controls, benefits, and information not available in the annual budget. The monthly budget enables the individual to observe the extent to which each month's receipts are sufficient to pay each month's expenses. Sometimes one may have to borrow (or save in advance) to meet financial needs on a month-to-month basis.

While the third phase--management of actual expenses--is not absolutely necessary, the more an individual plans and involves himself in the budget process, the better control he will have over his actual expenses. Each phase is explained and illustrated with a continuous example.

When compared to other budgeting processes, this approach requires a great deal more time in the early planning stages; however, it requires much less time from month to month. The schedules that you prepare will enable you to compare actual total monthly expenses and savings to projected total monthly expenses and savings. You do not need to record how you spend each dollar to gain control of your expenses. If after comparing these monthly payments you need more information, this system will provide it.

We have just previewed the final products of this manual and some of the ways they can be used to control expenses. For those who want to gain better control of their expenses so that they can purchase a house, get rid of anxiety, or just get more for their dollar, this manual can help achieve that goal.

Behavioral Considerations: Setting Priorities

Now that you know what the final product will be, how to use it, and how much time is required, I would like to comment on some of the behavioral aspects of personal budgeting.

Definition of Behavior

The word "behavior" is defined by *Webster's Seventh New Collegiate Dictionary* as "1: the manner of conducting oneself...." Our expenditure patterns can reveal our needs, our desires, our fears, and our frustrations. Our spending behavior, both what we buy and where we spend our money, is an integral part of who we are. As adults, our behavioral patterns are well established and, for most of us, would be extremely difficult to change. The budget process must recognize and accept these spending patterns. For example, some of us like expensive clothes while others enjoy playing golf. These spending preferences are deeply ingrained and must be accepted. This does not mean that unlimited amounts of money can be spent, but only that some provision should be made in the budget recognizing these preferences.

The people involved in the budgetary process must first accept their own spending habits and then those of others. Trying to ignore or change spending behavior is usually unproductive, but adjustments can be made when we identify what they are, and what their importance is to the quality of our lives. Another term for "identifying spending preferences" is "prioritizing" how we spend money.

Size of Group Prioritizing

The larger the group involved, the more difficult the process of prioritizing becomes. For example, with a family of four:

Individually

Priority	HUSBAND	WIFE	1st CHILD	2nd CHILD
1.				
2.				
3.				
4.				

Each individual should be able to list and rank individual activities; however, many of the activities may involve other members of the family.

Combinations

HUSBAND

Priority	HUSBAND WIFE	HUSBAND 1st CHILD	HUSBAND 2nd CHILD
1.			
2.			
3.			
4.			

WIFE

Priority	WIFE & 1st CHILD	WIFE & 2nd CHILD
1.		
2.		
3.		
4.		

CHILDREN

Priority	1st CHILD & 2nd CHILD
1.	
2.	
3.	
4.	

Husband and Wife

HUSBAND & WIFE Priority

1.
2.
3.
4.

HUSBAND/WIFE 1st CHILD	HUSBAND/WIFE 2nd CHILD

ENTIRE FAMILY Priority

1.
2.
3.
4.

ENTIRE FAMILY

Expenses to Be Prioritized

Which expenses should be prioritized. The expense classification and worksheets for this manual are organized around two major criteria. First, when are expenses made--annually or monthly?

1. Annual Expenses

Those expenses not incurred each month.
Examples: insurance
taxes
clothing
Christmas

2. Monthly Expenses

Those expenses incurred each month.
Examples: house payment
food
entertainment

Second, are they fixed or discretionary expenses? You have very little control over fixed expenses and probably would not be able to reduce them very much. With discretionary and operational expenses, however, you do have some degree of control and would be able to reduce them to some extent. Some examples are:

1. Annual

Fixed: insurance, taxes
Discretionary:
clothing
Christmas

2. Monthly

Fixed: house payment
Operational:
entertainment
food

If we consider that we have individual, combined, and family priorities, we would have the following expenses to prioritize.

Expense Categories Which Can Be Prioritized

By:	INDIVIDUAL	COMBINED	FAMILY
ANNUAL DISCRETIONARY			
Clothes	✓		
Household & Auto			✓
Medical & Dental	✓		
Christmas	✓	✓	✓
Subscriptions	✓	✓	
Vacation	✓		✓
MONTHLY OPERATIONAL			
Food			✓
Gas & Oil	✓	✓	✓
Entertainment	✓	✓	✓
Allowance	✓		
Miscellaneous	✓	✓	✓

Prioritize those expenses where you have the most control.

Budget First, Then Prioritize

To keep the process simple, your first budget (Phase 1) should incorporate reasonable estimates of your needs with no attempt to make any cuts or prioritize. The initial budget should represent what you would like to do and to spend. Only after preparing a budget which represents your real needs should you begin to prioritize. After preparation of the budget, how you do your ranking is an individual matter. Some years a family vacation may seem essential, while in other years, household purchases are more important. Some allowance for each family member may also be required.

Some of the prioritizing will represent specific needs. For example, money may be specifically set aside for storm windows. Other prioritizing will be represented by a "lump sum" dollar amount. Sometimes the easiest way to avoid problems is to grant everyone an amount to spend for individual priorities. This amount may be justified by a specific activity, like playing golf, but it should not be necessary for the individuals to account for how they spent the money. In order to prioritize for the family, priorities must be discussed. This process can be extremely difficult. If not handled properly, the entire budget procedure could fail. Below are two recommended approaches for identifying priorities.

Identifying Priorities

Acceptance of one's own spending preferences as well as others' is the major key to the success of the budget process. Two approaches to identifying priorities are:

1. If good communication exists and spending preferences have been discussed, the individuals may meet once or twice and simply list their priorities.

2. Where the above situation does not exist, the more elaborate process discussed below may be required.

In order to identify priorities, spending habits and patterns may need to be observed for several months. During this period, those involved should only note actual spending. It is important that they do not change spending patterns or preferences, or try to reduce spending.

The dollar expenditures recorded during this time should illustrate individual spending preferences and serve as the focal point of discussion where the prime objective is establishing and accepting individual priorities. It is recommended at this point that everyone record his observations about himself and about the others involved on a piece of paper, and then talk about them. These observations should be exchanged, with time allowed for reflection.

If necessary, written responses should also be prepared and shared. Open discussion should begin only when everyone is satisfied with the written exchanges. Failure to accept and arrive at some consensus on individual priorities will cause the budget process to fail. This is the most important step in the process, yet most people ignore it altogether. In summary, the identification of individual priorities may be completed immediately or it may require several months of observation. Individuals must communicate openly and honestly. Individuals must accept their own priority structures as well as the structures of others.

After the budget process begins, individuals may attempt to change their priority structures. People should have the flexibility to experiment with different spending patterns. Everyone should refrain from passing judgment on these attempts and what will at times result in failure to change. Finally, while the process is a serious one, maintaining a sense of humor will always increase the probability of success.

How to Avoid Potential Manipulation

During the discussion of priorities, an individual may try to "pad" by requesting more money than is necessary for a particular category. For example, a person may make a request for more clothing than he needs with the anticipation that he will later reduce his requests. Thus, his final list will represent what he actually needs, and he will have obtained what he wants without any true sacrifices. Further, he may try to use his apparent reduction as leverage to obtain consessions in other areas. For example, he may reduce his clothing request if his allowance is increased by one-half his clothing reduction. In this situation, his strategy would have yielded his true clothing needs and a greater allowance.

If everyone adopts this kind of strategy the process becomes very difficult and may break off entirely. To avoid this situation in negotiating cuts, do not allow trade-offs between categories, and try to instill an attitude of honesty in the process. This can be best accomplished by example. The one managing the finances must also make concessions in a category without reducing expenses in others. The sacrifices must be "real" and not cosmetic. Any attempt by the budget managers to manipulate the budget to their advantage will seriously undermine the budget process.

It is also important to remember that an atmosphere of respect and honesty must exist when working up a budget. If there are major problems between budget participants, a book or manual will not correct them. The parties involved must want to budget and must care for each other in order for this manual to be most effective.

Review: Setting Priorities

Priorities must be set during or after preparation of the first attempt at a budget. The first budget should represent true needs and can best be prepared in an atmosphere where everyone wants to budget and attempts to be honest. The discretionary and monthly operational expenses represent those expenses which can best be prioritized. Fixed annual and monthly expenses usually cannot be effectively controlled, and do not lend themselves to the prioritization process. The process appears complex because you have individual priorities, joint priorities, family priorities, and household priorities, but it is manageable. Individuals should identify:

1. Individual priorities--recommend a "lump sum."
2. Joint priorities--recommend a "lump sum."
3. Family priorities--recommend a "lump sum."

Once the budget is prepared, each individual should examine the budget and prepare a list of cuts based on his or her own priority structure. Do not consider household items and clothing until you see the entire budget. Some cuts will be directed towards specific items and some towards "lump sum" amounts. Some years one category will be important, and in other years another category will be more important. Those involved should meet to reach a consensus on which budget items should be reduced.

Importance of Prioritization to Our Family

My wife and I have been confronted on several occasions with decisions where the financial consequences could have caused major problems for our family. While working in industry, I decided to accept a teaching position, and as a result, my income was cut in half. Two years later when I went back to school, my income was halved again.

In allocating the very slim budget, however, we were careful to take account of our spending priorities because we knew that if we didn't, our budget could be destroyed. For instance, we always allocated a small amount for entertainment. Although our income was small, we recognized that both of us needed to go out occasionally, so we put it into the budget.

Later, when I returned from graduate school to teaching, prioritization helped us make another decision. We had never bought living room furniture, and much of what we had was given to us when we were first married.

For two years we put money aside until we had saved \$3,500. During this same period, we had also talked about taking an extended trip through the West. Weighing such things as our longing for a kind of "renewal" and the children's ages against our need for the furniture, we decided on the trip.

These were critical decisions which could have resulted in a great deal of pressure for my family. We were able to minimize the negative impact for three reasons. First, my wife and I were committed to our marriage and these decisions. Second, we have always been committed to living within our income, and third, we were able to recognize priorities and effectively manage them.

Selecting the Budget Preparer

This budget manual has not been prepared to accommodate any particular "family management style" or family situation. The manual may be used by anyone interested in budgeting effectively.

Whatever style used, it is recommended that one person be responsible for putting the numbers together, preferably the one who would enjoy the job and who has the necessary skills.

Summary of the Budget Process

1. Select individual to prepare budget.
2. Prepare annual budget (Phase 1).
3. Identify priorities while preparing budget.
4. Adjust budget based on agreed-upon priorities.
5. Allocate annual budget on a monthly basis (Phase 2).
6. Manage budget on a monthly basis based on prepared schedules (Phase 3).

Chapter 2

Phase 1: Preparation of The Annual Budget

Introduction

The next page is a summary of how Phase 1 is structured and how the information flows from the various worksheets to the final product--the Budget Summary (AB-12). Note that AB represents Annual Budget. You should take time to examine each of the seven steps and look at the forms to trace the estimated annual fixed expenses, annual discretionary (Forms AB-2, -3, -4, -5, -6, -7) to AB-8, a summarization of all annual expenses. Note that the total of AB-8 is transferred to Form AB-12. It is important that you understand what the end product is for Phase 1 (AB-12, the Annual Budget)--and how it is put together, before you begin. All totals from the various forms should be traced through to the final budget before starting.

The four major expense categories are:

1.	Annual Fixed	Form AB-1	Step 1
2.	Annual Discretionary and	Form AB-2 - AB-7	Step 2
	Summarization on	Form AB-8	Step 3
3.	Monthly Fixed	Form AB-9	Step 4
4.	Monthly Operational	Form AB-10	Step 5
	Revenue is computed on	Form AB-11	Step 6
	The budget is summarized on	Form AB-12	Step 7

The next page provides a more extensive and complete overview.

Phase 1--Overview

Step	Form	Form Total	Form AB-12	Line No. AB-12
1. Estimate annual fixed expense	AB-1	$ 2,355*	$ 2,355	2
2. Estimate annual discretionary expense				
Clothes	AB-2	$ 2,450		
Household & auto	AB-3	1,670		
Medical & dental	AB-4	450		
Christmas	AB-5	985		
Subscriptions	AB-6	89		
Vacation	AB-6	1,200		
Uncertain	AB-7	350		
3. Summarize annual discretionary expense Total Forms AB-2 through AB-7	AB-8	$ 7,194*	+$ 7,194	7
4. Estimate monthly fixed expenses and annualize	AB-9	$ 5,328*	+$ 5,328	3
5. Estimate monthly operational expenses and annualize	AB-10	$10,800*	+$10,800	4
Total annual expenses			$25,677	
6. Estimate annual receipts Deduct annual expenses to obtain amount for Step 7:	AB-11	$25,527*	-$25,527	
7. Estimate annual budget	AB-12		$ -150	8

*These amounts are transferred to Form AB-12, the Annual Budget.

General Procedure for Phase 1

Before estimating each expense, gather together sources of past years' payments which would typically include:

Checkbook and check stubs

Canceled checks

Paid bills

Insurance policies

Federal, state, and local tax returns

The mechanical process for budgeting each expense is somewhat similar. The basic approach follows:

1. Define expense.
2. List some of the items that belong in the category.
3. Examine and list the amount spent in the past. (Complete this step only if information is readily available.)
4. Determine the quantity, if necessary, and the dollar amount to be spent this year.
5. Adjust for inflation and increased costs if necessary.
6. Add behavioral comments.
7. Transfer to Summary Sheet.

Remember: Your first attempt at a budget should incorporate a reasonable estimate of your needs with <u>no</u> attempt to make cuts or to prioritize.

STEP 1: ANNUAL EXPENSES--FIXED (FORM AB-1)

Definition: Annual fixed expenses are those expenses which a person would hesitate to reduce or eliminate. They are not paid on a monthly basis. Some may be paid once a year, others several times a year.

Items included in this category:

1. Property tax
2. Property insurance
3. Auto insurance
4. Life insurance
5. Disability insurance
6. Dues
7. Any other expense which fits the above definition

List amount spent last year: List date of payment using checkbook and paid bills if available. (See form on next page.)

Determine quantity and amount for this year: Use last year's expense and adjust accordingly.

Adjust for potential cost increase:

1. Source: Call local auditor or assessment office; estimate your own potential costs based on prior year's increases; consider general inflation rate--check local newspapers, Wall Street Journal, Time, Newsweek, Forbes magazines.

2. Computation: For example, assume an 8% (.08) increase this year for an item costing $300 last year. $300 x 1.08 = $324 estimated cost this year.

3. My basis for the example: I increased each of the expenses by an amount I considered reasonable--this method often called "seat-of-pants."

Behavioral comments: It is difficult to reduce costs here unless a major reduction is required. As a result, there are very few behavioral consequences.

Transfer to Summary Sheet: In my example, transfer the $2,355 on Form AB-1 to Form AB-12 on page 51, line 2.

FORM AB-1

ANNUAL EXPENSES--FIXED

EXPENSE CATEGORY	PAYMENT MONTH(S)	LAST YEAR'S COST	THIS YEAR'S COST	NO. OF PAY-MENTS	TOTAL COST THIS YEAR
Property Tax *	Jan, July	$ 350	$ 390	2	$ 780
Property Insurance	Aug	$ 240	$ 300	1	$ 300
Auto Insurance:					
Vega	Feb, Aug	$ 140	$ 150	2	$ 300
Olds	March, Sep	$ 160	$ 170	2	$ 340
Life Insurance	October	$ 275	$ 275	1	$ 275
Disability Insurance	July	$ 190	$ 210	1	$ 210
Dues:					
AAA	Jan	$ 25	$ 35	1	$ 35
AICPA	July	$ 35	$ 40	1	$ 40
Ohio CPA	May	$ 55	$ 60	1	$ 60
CPA License	March	$ 15	$ 15	1	$ 15
TOTAL	(Put total on Form AB-12, page 51 line 2.)				$2,355
	*See note about property tax on Form AB-9, page 45.				

STEP 2: ANNUAL EXPENSES--DISCRETIONARY

I have labeled my forms as listed below. You may use these five categories or others based on your specific needs.

Item	Form	Page
Clothes	AB-2	31
Household & Auto	AB-3	33
Medical & Dental	AB-4	35
Christmas	AB-5	37
Other	AB-6	39
Uncertain	AB-7	41

Definition: Discretionary annual expenses are not incurred on a monthly basis. They represent necessary and desirable expenses; however, often there is some discretion about the amount that a person may want to spend in a category. These expenditures offer opportunities for budget cuts and, as a result, have many behavioral implications. Priorities must be established to make effective workable budget deductions.

For each of these categories and forms, I have (1) listed items included in the category; (2) listed the amount spent last year; (3) listed the quantity and amount this year; (4) adjusted for potential cost increase; (5) made behavioral comments; and (6) transferred amounts to the Summary Sheet.

Annual Expenses--Discretionary Clothes (Form AB-2)

Items included in category: Each member of the family is listed along with how he or she views clothing purchases. For me, work and leisure represent the two major categories. For the remaining members of the family the seasons are more appropriate.

List amount spent last year: This may be difficult to accomplish. You may have to examine closets to note items which were gifts. You may have to guess the amount. If this task becomes too difficult, leave last year's column blank.

Determine quantity and amount for this year: How the quantity for each individual is determined depends on the management style of the budget preparer. The preparer may independently determine each individual's needs without seeking advice or he may want people to participate. When he invites participation, he should encourage people to examine the condition of their clothes and note special occasions such as dances, dinners, and trips. Each person should first list the items and then estimate the cost.

Adjust for potential cost increase: Not applicable here since different items are probably being purchased. Where the items are not listed but a dollar amount is determined, you may want to take last year's dollars and adjust upwards based on the inflation rate. For an example of this type of computation, see "Computation" in Step 1: Annual Expenses--Fixed.

Behavioral comments: This area is open to the potential of "padding," as discussed in the behavioral section in the introduction. Because clothing is such a substantial item, I find that I must periodically (once every three months) review clothing needs with everyone.

Transfer to Summary Sheet: Transfer the $2,450 to AB-8 on page 43.

FORM AB-2

ANNUAL EXPENSES--DISCRETIONARY

CLOTHES

EXPENSE CATEGORY	LAST YEAR	THIS YEAR	REVISIONS			
			1	2	3	4
Harper						
Work	$ 225	$ 250				
Leisure	$ 250	$ 250				
SUBTOTAL #1	$ 475	$ 500				
Sally						
Fall	$ 125	$ 150				
Holidays	$ 125	$ 150				
Spring	$ 125	$ 100				
Summer	$ 150	$ 200				
SUBTOTAL #2	$ 525	$ 600				
Drew						
Fall	$ 100	$ 250				
Winter	$ 100	$ 250				
Spring/Summer	$ 150	$ 100				
SUBTOTAL #3	$ 350	$ 600				
Jane						
Fall	$ 200	$ 250				
Winter	$ 200	$ 250				
Spring/Summer	$ 200	$ 250				
SUBTOTAL #4	$ 600	$ 750				
TOTAL OF						
SUBTOTALS	$1,950	$2,450	(Put total on AB-8, page 43.)			

Annual Expenses--Discretionary Household & Auto--Replacement (Form AB-3)

Items included in category: This expense category has three types: (1) expenses necessary to maintain current lifestyle; (2) expenses which will cut operational costs (storm windows); and (3) expenses which will improve standard of living. Examples of items include small appliances, furniture, T.V.s, planned car repair, exterior house repair and maintenance, and major appliances. The expenses in this area are planned.

List amount spent last year: I do not list last year's amounts, but list items from last year to remind me what has been done so I can project more accurately what might need to be budgeted. The planned expenses in this area include: tires for Oldsmobile, insulation for house, new dishwasher, T.V. for family room. In addition, I review items which were not planned for from form AB-7, page 41, motor, exhaust for Vega, tires for Vega, wiring for Vega.

Determine quantity and amount for this year: Using the three areas (1) maintain, (2) cut costs, (3) improve, I list items at the bottom of AB-3 with a dollar amount.

Adjust for potential cost increases: I attempt to obtain realistic amounts by calling various services and asking neighbors.

Behavioral comments: The order of priority is (1) maintain, (2) cut costs, and (3) improve. All of the items in this category are planned for in advance and represent expenditures that I would *like* to incur. Most of the time, a great deal of discretion exists as to when these costs will be incurred and paid. Usually they can be postponed for at least six months.

Transfer to Summary Sheet: The $1,670 on the bottom of AB-3 should be transferred to AB-8, page 43.

FORM AB-3

ANNUAL EXPENSES--DISCRETIONARY

HOUSEHOLD & AUTO--REPLACEMENT

LAST YEAR ACTUAL		REVISIONS 1	2	3	4	5
Tires -- Olds Insulation Dishwasher T.V. -- Family						
THIS YEAR PLANNED						
MAINTAIN:						
Paint House Car Tune-Up: Vega Olds Garage Door	\$ 250 \$ 50 \$ 120 \$ 500					
CUT COSTS:						
Storm Windows (½ windows)	\$ 500					
IMPROVE:						
Garage Door Opener	\$ 250					
TOTAL	\$1,670	(Put total on AB-8, page 43.)				

Annual Expenses--Discretionary
Medical & Dental (Form AB-4)

Items included in category: Physical examinations, dental exams, planned dental work, and medicine. I list one medicine category for the entire family.

List amount spent last year: See Form AB-4 on next page. The amount recorded should only be what you pay in excess of any insurance reimbursements.

Determine quantity and amount this year: A physical exam for each of us (4) and two dental cleanings and examinations for each of us (8).

Adjust for any potential cost increase: Do not be embarrassed to call both your doctor's and dentist's office to inquire about fees for this year.

Behavioral comments: Two comments. The first is a personal note. Neither my wife nor I had regular physical examinations until we started budgeting. Budgeting can be a way to cause some positive changes in your life. Second, I know many people who might be classified as hypochondriacs. It is very important that no one prejudge any of the other budget participants. When the budget is completed, the dollar amount that anyone spends in a given category including health care will be evident to everyone.

Transfer to Summary Sheet: The $450 on the bottom of AB-4 should be transferred to AB-8, page 43.

FORM AB-4

ANNUAL EXPENSES--DISCRETIONARY

MEDICAL AND DENTAL

EXPENSE CATEGORY	LAST YEAR	THIS YEAR	REVISIONS 1	2	3	4
Harper						
Medical	$ 100	$ 120				
Dental	$ 50*	$ 50				
Sally						
Medical	$ 100	$ 120				
Dental						
Drew						
Medical	$ 40	$ 50				
Dental						
Jane						
Medical	$ 40	$ 50				
Dental						
Medicine	$ 30	$ 60				
TOTAL	$ 360	$ 450	(Put total on AB-8, page 43.)			
	*Insurance covers all but $50 of dental and most medical expenses except for physicals and visits to the doctor.					

Annual Expenses--Discretionary
Christmas (Form AB-5)

Items included in category: I list each person for whom I intend to purchase a Christmas present. In addition, I include an extra amount for other holiday activities.

List amount spent last year: Usually, I must review this with my wife.

Determine quantity and amount this year: I review with my wife the list of people she intends to include for the coming year. I always ask her what she thinks will be a reasonable amount for various people.

Adjust for any potential cost increase: The increase in the cost of various items is always an integral part of the discussion of what is going to be a "reasonable amount" for this year.

Behavioral comments: At first, my wife felt that this procedure was too calculated and spoiled some of the atmosphere of Christmas. She now appreciates the need for estimating the dollars. If we know in advance the amount to be spent, we can more easily adjust. Further, I am always able to pay Christmas bills when due--not throughout the year at 18% interest.

Transfer to Summary Sheet: The $985 on the bottom of AB-5 should be transferred to AB-8, page 43.

FORM AB-5

ANNUAL EXPENSES--DISCRETIONARY

CHRISTMAS

EXPENSE CATEGORY	LAST YEAR	THIS YEAR	REVISIONS			
			1	2	3	4
Family						
Harper	$ 125	$ 150				
Sally	$ 125	$ 150				
Drew	$ 75	$ 100				
Jane	$ 75	$ 100				
Sal's Family						
Mill	$ 35	$ 40				
Carl	$ 35	$ 40				
Bee	$ 35	$ 40				
Mary	$ 20	$ 25				
Noah	$ 20	$ 25				
Harp's Family						
Alice	$ 35	$ 40				
Sis	$ 20	$ 25				
Additional for						
travel, etc.	$ 200	$ 250				
TOTAL	$ 800	$ 985	(Put total on AB-8, page 43.)			

Annual Expenses--Discretionary Other (Form AB-6)

Items included in category: Include all other annual discretionary expenses that do not have a special sheet. I listed subscriptions and vacation.

List amount spent last year: The checkbook stubs should be a good source for subscription costs. For vacation, I listed what I thought we had spent which included gas, room, food, and incidentals in excess of the normal operational cost money that is available during that time. In other words, I spent more than $1,000; however, I spent $1,000 in addition to what had been available for normal living costs.

Determine quantity and amount this year: For subscriptions, I review with the family the magazines they would like to receive and estimate the increase. For vacation, we discuss some possibilities of places to visit and approximately how much time will be spent. The number of days is the most important element for estimating vacation costs. We never finalize specific vacation plans at this time; however, we budget dollars based on the approximate length of vacation. The elements should include car preparation, gas, oil, lodging, and food. If you have no idea of travel costs, AAA can assist you if you are a member.

Adjust for any potential cost increase: Not applicable.

Behavioral comments: Often people preparing a budget will attempt to reduce expenses by eliminating the vacation from the budget. If you are accustomed to vacations and they are important to you, include a reasonable amount for a vacation in your initial budget. A vacation should be included with all other expenses when prioritizing.

Transfer to Summary Sheet: The $88.50 for subscriptions and the $1,200 for vacation on AB-6 are transferred to AB-8, page 43.

FORM AB-6

ANNUAL EXPENSES--DISCRETIONARY

OTHER

EXPENSE CATEGORY	LAST YEAR	THIS YEAR	REVISIONS 1	2	3	4
Subscriptions:						
Time	$ 31.00	$ 36.00				
(November)						
Sports	$ 24.00	$ 28.00				
Illustrated						
(December)						
Ladies Home	$ 14.50	$ 16.00				
Journal						
(August)						
National	$ 7.50	$ 8.50				
Geographic						
(July)						
TOTAL	$ 77.00	$ 88.50	(Put total on AB-8, page 43.)			
Vacation:						
Michigan		$ 900.00				
Convention		$ 300.00				
TOTAL	$1,000.00	$1,200.00	(Put total on AB-8, page 43.)			

Annual Expenses--Discretionary Uncertain (Form AB-7)

Items included in category: Each year there are required expenditures which have not been anticipated, planned, or covered by insurance. I list specific components of the car and specific items and areas within the household. Form AB-7, on the next page, provides a more complete list. Your list may include other items.

List amount spent last year: I list the dollar amount of the "uncertain" expenses for last year and examine last year's AB-3, Household & Auto.

Determine quantity and amount this year: It is impossible to budget for this area by specific item. I tend to develop a sense for what will happen by examining last year's and this year's planned household AB-3 and previous year's uncertain expenses on Form AB-7. I always budget slightly more than the amount from the previous year, mainly because of inflation.

Adjust for any potential cost increase: No specific approach--just by "seat-of-pants."

Behavioral comments: As you budget for the planned area (AB-3) and note uncertain expenses (AB-7), you become more aware of the physical condition and needs of your household. As a result, eventually fewer uncertain events occur.

Transfer to Summary Sheet: The $350 on the bottom of AB-7 should be transferred to AB-8, page 43.

FORM AB-7

ANNUAL EXPENSES--DISCRETIONARY

UNCERTAIN

EXPENSE CATEGORY	LAST YEAR	THIS YEAR	REVISIONS			
			1	2	3	4
Automobile						
Motor	$ 150					
Exhaust						
Electric	$ 50					
General						
Tire	$ 42					
SUBTOTAL	$ 242					
Household						
Plumbing	$ 50					
Window						
Stove						
Refrigerator						
Furnace						
Lawn						
Dishwasher						
T.V.s						
Other						
SUBTOTAL	$ 50					
Medical						
Dental						
TOTAL	$ 292	$ 350	(Put total on AB-8, page 43.)			

STEP 3: SUMMARY OF ANNUAL DISCRETIONARY EXPENSES--(FORM AB-8)

All of the annual discretionary expenses (Forms AB-2 to AB-7) are included on Form AB-8 with the total transferred to AB-12 on page 51, line 7.

FORM AB-8

PRELIMINARY SUMMARY OF ANNUAL DISCRETIONARY EXPENSES

EXPENSE CATEGORY	THIS YEAR	REVISIONS 1	2	3	4
Annual					
Discretionary					
Forms:					
Clothes	$2,450				
(AB-2)					
House & Auto	$1,670				
(AB-3)					
Medical	$ 450				
(AB-4)					
Christmas	$ 985				
(AB-5)					
Subscriptions	$ 89				
(AB-6)					
Vacation	$1,200				
(AB-6)					
Uncertain	$ 350				
(AB-7)					
TOTAL	$7,194	(Put total on AB-12, page 51, line 7.)			

STEP 4: MONTHLY FIXED EXPENSES--(FORM AB-9)

Definition: Monthly fixed expenses represent items which must be paid monthly or where the amount can be averaged each month.

Items included in category: House payment, church pledge, telephone, water and sewage, electric and gas, and any other expense which must be paid monthly.

List amount spent last year: See Form AB-9. Sources include mortgage agreement, mortgage payment book, church records, the utility company, past bills.

Determine quantity and amount this year: House payment--remains constant unless you have a variable interest rate mortgage. Church--determined by individual. Telephone--a review of past long-distance phone expenses and normal charges. Water and sewage, electric and gas--not much opportunity for adjustment unless something major develops (storm windows, family member leaves home, etc.).

Adjust for any potential cost increase: For telephone, water and sewage, electric and gas, the utility's business office should be able to provide the approximate cost increase percentage. I usually estimate without calling and through the years have become a fairly accurate projector.

Behavioral comments: Much has been written about conservation in the area of utility consumption. If you have not already made some adjustments, you should talk with the various utility companies. Most firms have literature and programs available. If you have employed cost-saving measures, any reductions beyond those already accepted probably will not be effective because they would require major behavioral modifications.

Transfer to Summary Sheet: The $5,328 annual monthly fixed expenses should be transferred to AB-12, page 51, line 3.

FORM AB-9

MONTHLY-FIXED EXPENSES

EXPENSE CATEGORY	LAST YEAR	THIS YEAR	REVISIONS 1	2	3
House Payment *	$ 218.75	$ 218.75			
Church	$ 45.00	$ 50.00			
Telephone	$ 25.00	$ 30.00			
Water & Sewer	$ 40.00	$ 45.00			
Electric & Gas	$ 90.00	$ 100.00			
TOTAL	$ 424.00	$ 444.00			
MONTHLY EXPENSE		$ 444.00			
NUMBER OF MONTHS		x 12			
ANNUAL EXPENSE		$5,328.00	(Put total on AB-12, line 3, page 51.)		

*Note: On Form AB-1, the first item listed is property tax. I pay my own property tax with a check twice a year. Many banks and lending institutions provide a service in which the house payment and property taxes are deducted directly from an individual's checking account. If this service is being provided, the property tax payment will be included under fixed monthly expenses and not annual fixed expenses.

STEP 5: MONTHLY OPERATIONAL EXPENSES (FORM AB-10)

Definition Monthly Operational Expenses: Monthly operational expenses represent expenses incurred on a monthly basis which are, for the most part, considered essential; however, for some of the areas, individuals have a great deal of control.

Items included in category:
Food--includes all household items (soap, shampoo, or anything which can be purchased at the grocery store).
Gas and oil.
Entertainment--includes consideration of family priority items such as fast food, dining out, movies, sporting events, and theater.
Children--includes lunch money.
Allowance--each member is granted a lump sum amount and is not held accountable.
Miscellaneous--includes all other monthly expenses. This amount, in part, should be used to pay for unexpected items and events which would be considered high priority. For example, a family member wants everyone to go see the "Reds" play that evening--an event not scheduled for that month. In other words, you should attempt to provide a "lump sum" amount in the miscellaneous category for this kind of "spur-of-the-moment" activity.

Determine quantity and amount this year: Food--observe what you think you will need; gas and oil--estimate number of fillings per month. For example:

	Fillings per month		Gallons		Total		Price per gallon	Total
Vega	2	x	12	=	24	x	$ 1.25	=$ 30.00
Olds	4	x	21	=	84	x	$ 1.30	=$109.20
								$139.20
							Oil and other	10.80
							projected expenses	$150.00

Entertainment--estimate with no particular basis.
Children's lunch--number of school days multiplied by lunch cost.
Allowance--must be sufficient to allow some of individual's priorities.
Miscellaneous--do not estimate too low.

Adjust for any potential cost increase: Not applicable.

Behavioral comments: My objective is to determine a lump sum for operating the household during the month. I am not too concerned where I spend the money. When I must reduce expenses, I prefer to indicate which category of expenses will be affected. For the first month or so, I use envelopes to hold money for various categories. This procedure can only work for one or two months. It helps me to determine if the total monthly amount is sufficient and, if not, where adjustments are required. I never record how I spend money on a monthly or daily basis.

Transfer to Summary Sheet: The $10,800 on Form AB-10 should be transferred to Form AB-12, page 51, line 4.

FORM AB-10

MONTHLY-OPERATIONAL EXPENSES

EXPENSE CATEGORY	LAST YEAR	THIS YEAR	REVISIONS 1	2	3
Food	$ 350	$ 400			
Gas & Oil	$ 150	$ 150			
Entertainment	$ 100	$ 100			
Kids Lunch	$ 40	$ 40			
Allowance*	$ 70	$ 85			
Miscellaneous	$ 90	$ 125			
MONTHLY TOTAL	$ 800	$ 900			
MONTHLY EXPENSE		$ 900			
NUMBER OF MONTHS		x 12			
ANNUAL EXPENSES		$10,800	(Transfer to AB-12, page 51, line 4.)		

Allowance:	Last Year	This Year
Jane	$ 10	$ 10
Drew	$ 10	$ 15
Sal	$ 25	$ 30
Harp	$ 25	$ 30
TOTAL	$ 70	$ 85

STEP 6: COMPUTATION OF TAKE-HOME PAY AND CASH RECEIPTS (FORM AB-11)

The following information is provided to illustrate the procedure on the next page:

1. Last year's gross wages, $30,586.
2. Estimated range for this year's salary increase amount--5% to 9%.
3. Last year's net monthly take-home pay was $1,988.
4. Last year's gross monthly wages were $2,548.
5. No additional sources of outside income.

Special note for item 5, Form AB-11: Reduce estimated take-home pay by anticipated additional taxes. This information can be obtained from last year's federal, state, and local income tax returns. If, in the past, additional taxes have been paid, it is a good assumption that additional taxes will have to be paid in the future. I usually estimate an amount based on past experience.

Transfer $25,527 from Form AB-11 to Form AB-12, page 51, line 1.

FORM AB-11

COMPUTATION OF CASH RECEIPTS FOR COMING YEAR

1. Estimate range of annual salary increment and use midpoint to increase.

   For Example: 5% to 9% -- Average = 7%

2. Increase gross wages by average percentage.

   Last Year's Gross Wages: $30,586 x 107% = $32,727

3. Compute take-home percentage (use last year's payroll check stubs).

   Last Year's Net : $1,988 ÷ $2,548 = 78.02%

   Last Year's Gross : $2,548

4. Multiply take-home percentage (line 3) times estimated gross wages this year (line 2).

$32,727 x 78% (from above, rounded)	=	$ 25,527
5. Reduce by any additional anticipated taxes.	=	-0-
6. Add: Any additional sources of income	=	
and		-0-
7. Deduct: Any taxes which will be due	=	
8. Estimated Total Cash Receipt	=	$ 25,527 *

* Transfer amount to AB-12, page 51, line 1.

STEP 7: ANNUAL BUDGET SUMMARY (FORM AB-12)

The Annual Budget Summary, Form AB-12, is structured so that you can observe to what extent you control your expenses.

Line 6. $7,044 cash available for discretionary expenses indicates:

1. your cash receipts provided for most essential expenses.
2. You control when and how you spend a large percentage of your income.

Line 8. An adjustment ($150) or reduction is required in order for cash receipts to equal cash expenses.

Line 10. A $1,350 reduction in expenses is required to meet our savings goal.

The Annual Budget should be adjusted before preparing a monthly budget.

BUDGET SUMMARY--ANNUAL

LINE		THIS YEAR	REVISIONS 1	REVISIONS 2
1. Annual Cash Receipts		$ 25,527		
Add:				
2. Annual Fixed Expenses	+	$ 2,355		
3. Monthly Fixed Expenses	+	$ 5,328		
4. Monthly Operational Expenses	+	$ 10,800		
5. Total (lines 2, 3, 4)		$ 18,483		
Deduct: line 5 from line 1 (Annual Cash Receipts) to get line 6				
6. Cash Available for Discretionary Expenses		$ 7,044		
7. Deduct Discretionary Expenses	-	$ 7,194		
8. Total Cash Available After All Expenses				
Cash Excess				
Cash Short ( )		$ (150)		
9. Deduct Desired Savings		$ (1,200)		
10. Required Adjustment		$ (1,350)		

REVISION OF BUDGET

General Approach

At this point, the members of the family who are going to participate in the budget process should have discussed and identified, in a general sense, the following priorities:

Individual	
Combination	May have discussed some "lump sum" which seems appropriate.
Family	
Some specific household item	

In the reduction process, my family discusses both personal and group priorities and what amounts might be appropriate for each. When we agree, the budget is adjusted. If each member accepts the budget and feels that he or she is a part of the process, the budget has a much better chance for success.

How you make the adjustments is an individual matter, but it is important that individual priorities are recognized. Comments like "she is nuts over shoes," "she's an uncontrollable spender," "he is a clothes horse," or "he spends a fortune on golf," are not helpful. Usually these expressions are made to ridicule. We must learn to accept others' idiosyncrasies as well as our own. The budget should make some provision for our personal spending preferences like a lump-sum allowance. If this is <u>not</u> done, the budget will more than likely be a success. It may be necessary to follow the detailed procedure outlined earlier to accomplish this recognition and acceptance. A budget should not be implemented until the individual priorities have been identified and accepted.

Adjustments

In this particular example, the budget expenses almost equal budgeted revenue with nothing available for savings. This initial budget seems to exemplify the universal, "I can just barely meet expenses, but I cannot save anything."

My family and I discuss various aspects of the budget and potential reductions: clothing, Christmas gifts, vacation, and household expenses.

In the initial attempt to reduce expenses, we would probably make adjustments to the annual discretionary expenses first, and then, monthly operational expenses.

Clothing:		
Me	$ 50	
Sal	100	
Drew	100	
Jane	100	
Subtotal	350	(AB-2)
Door opener	250	(AB-3)
Christmas	150	(AB-5)
Reduction in annual discretionary expense	750	
Total reduction in monthly operational	600	= 12 x $50 per month (AB-10)
Total expense reduction	$1,350	

In order to obtain a $50 reduction in the monthly operation ($900 to $850), we agreed that entertainment should be reduced $20 and miscellaneous should be reduced $30 per month.

We will attempt to live within this budget with the understanding that in the next few months if we find it too difficult and unpleasant, we must adjust the budget in other ways.

During this time, I use the envelopes and will continue using them until we have what appears to be an acceptable budget. The current budget allows us (not in priority order) to:

1. Continue the same level of health care.
2. Maintain the physical condition of the house.
3. Provide for a vacation.
4. Maintain an individual discretionary fund for me and Sal.
5. Provide for monthly entertainment.
6. Maintain charitable contributions.
7. Provide $1,200 savings.
8. Maintain a $350 contingency fund for the year.

It is important to note the positive aspects of your budget for the entire family. Pages 56 through 61 illustrate the adjustments and the forms that need to be changed.

FORM AB-2

ANNUAL EXPENSES--DISCRETIONARY

CLOTHES

EXPENSE CATEGORY	LAST YEAR	THIS YEAR	REVISIONS 1	2	3	4
Harper						
Work	$ 225	$ 250	$ 225			
Leisure	$ 250	$ 250	$ 225			
SUBTOTAL #1	$ 475	$ 500	$ 450			
Sally						
Fall	$ 125	$ 150	$ 125			
Holidays	$ 125	$ 150	$ 125			
Spring	$ 125	$ 100	$ 100			
Summer	$ 150	$ 200	$ 150			
SUBTOTAL #2	$ 525	$ 600	$ 500			
Drew						
Fall	$ 100	$ 250	$ 200			
Winter	$ 100	$ 250	$ 200			
Spring/Summer	$ 150	$ 100	$ 100			
SUBTOTAL #3	$ 350	$ 600	$ 500			
Jane						
Fall	$ 200	$ 250	$ 200			
Winter	$ 200	$ 250	$ 200			
Spring/Summer	$ 200	$ 250	$ 250			
SUBTOTAL #4	$ 600	$ 750	$ 650			
TOTAL OF SUBTOTALS	$1,950	$2,450	$2,100	(Put total on AB-8, page 59, column 1.)		

FORM AB-3

ANNUAL EXPENSES--DISCRETIONARY

HOUSEHOLD & AUTO--REPLACEMENT

LAST YEAR ACTUAL		REVISIONS 1	2	3	4	5
Tires — Olds						
Insulation						
Dishwasher						
T.V. — Family						
THIS YEAR PLANNED						
MAINTAIN:						
Paint House	$ 250	$ 250				
Car Tune-Up:						
Vega	$ 50	$ 50				
Olds	$ 120	$ 120				
Garage Door	$ 500	$ 500				
CUT COSTS:						
Storm Windows (½ windows)	$ 500	$ 500				
IMPROVE:						
Garage Door Opener	$ 250	$ -0-				
TOTAL	$1,670	$1,420	(Put total on AB-8, page 59, column 1.)			

FORM AB-5

ANNUAL EXPENSES--DISCRETIONARY

CHRISTMAS

EXPENSE CATEGORY	LAST YEAR	THIS YEAR	REVISIONS			
			1	2	3	4
Family						
Harper	$ 125	$ 150	$ 135			
Sally	$ 125	$ 150	$ 135			
Drew	$ 75	$ 100	$ 90			
Jane	$ 75	$ 100	$ 90			
Sal's Family						
Mill	$ 35	$ 40	$ 35			
Carl	$ 35	$ 40	$ 35			
Bee	$ 35	$ 40	$ 35			
Mary	$ 20	$ 25	$ 25			
Noah	$ 20	$ 25	$ 25			
Harp's Family						
Alice	$ 35	$ 40	$ 35			
Sis	$ 20	$ 25	$ 25			
Additional for						
travel, etc.	$ 200	$ 250	$ 170			
TOTAL	$ 800	$ 985	$ 835	(Put total on AB-8, page 59, column 1.)		

FORM AB-8

PRELIMINARY SUMMARY OF ANNUAL DISCRETIONARY EXPENSES

EXPENSE CATEGORY	THIS YEAR	REVISIONS 1	2	3	4
Annual					
Discretionary					
Forms:					
Clothes	$2,400	$2,100			
(AB-2)					
House & Auto	$1,670	$1,420			
(AB-3)					
Medical	$ 450	$ 450			
(AB-4)					
Christmas	$ 985	$ 835			
(AB-5)					
Subscriptions	$ 89	$ 89			
(AB-6)					
Vacation	$1,200	$1,200			
(AB-6)					
Uncertain	$ 350	$ 350			
(AB-7)					
TOTAL	$7,194	$6,444	(Put total on AB-12, page 61, column 2, line 7.)		

FORM AB-10

MONTHLY--OPERATIONAL

EXPENSE CATEGORY	LAST YEAR	THIS YEAR	REVISIONS		
			1	2	3
Food	$ 350	$ 400	$ 400		
Gas & Oil	$ 150	$ 150	$ 150		
Entertainment	$ 100	$ 100	$ 80		
Kids (Lunch)	$ 40	$ 40	$ 40		
Allowance	$ 70	$ 85	$ 85		
Miscellaneous	$ 90	$ 125	$ 95		
MONTHLY TOTAL	$ 800	$ 900	$ 850		
MONTHLY EXPENSE			$ 850		
NUMBER OF MONTHS			x 12		
ANNUAL EXPENSES			$10,200	(Put total on AB-12, page 61, column 2, line 4.)	

FORM AB-12

BUDGET SUMMARY--ANNUAL

LINE		THIS YEAR	REVISIONS 1	REVISIONS 2
1. Annual Cash Receipts		$ 25,527	$ 25,527	
Add:				
2. Annual Fixed Expenses	+	$ 2,355	$ 2,355	
3. Monthly Fixed Expenses	+	$ 5,328	$ 5,328	
4. Monthly Operational Expenses	+	$ 10,800	$ 10,200	
5. Total (lines 2, 3, 4)		$ 18,483	$ 17,883	
Deduct: line 5 from line 1 (Annual Cash Receipts) to get line 6				
6. Cash Available for Discretionary Expenses		$ 7,044	$ 7,644	
7. Deduct Discretionary Expenses	-	$ 7,194	$ 6,444	
8. Total Cash Available After All Expenses				
Cash Excess			$ 1,200	
Cash Short ( )		$ (150)		
9. Deduct Desired Savings		$ (1,200)	$ (1,200)	
10. Required Adjustment		$ (1,350)	$ -0-	

What About Situations Where Large Debt Exists?

In our family we have saved cash for every purchase except the house and car. We have a rule that every charge account must be paid in full each month. Only when the charge is interest free do we extend payments beyond thirty days. The policy is not just financially conservative, it relieves a great deal of psychological pressure in the household.

How did we get into this position? We started our married life this way. However, if you have a large amount of consumer credit, you can begin immediately working towards a complete elimination of this short-term debt. You can substitute debt payment in place of savings within the structure provided. For the individual who is accustomed to acquiring items by time payments, this will be very difficult. The credit habit is addictive.

The only method I know of eliminating this problem altogether is to attempt to save something and to purchase items for cash while you are eliminating your debt. The cycle of cash-to-purchase is psychologically more rewarding than the cycle of purchase-to-payment-plus-interest. A person may need counseling during this time if uncontrolled spending behavior is deeply entrenched.

Summary of Phase 1

Phase 1 enables the budget preparer and those affected to observe where money is being spent and for what activities. Should something happen to the budget preparer, this annual budget would provide valuable information to those who might suddenly be thrust into a position of financial responsibility. All receipts and a very detailed list of expenditures would be provided. While it is not absolutely necessary to prepare Phases 2 and 3, the second phase only requires the use of three forms and arranging Phase-1 data into a monthly format. Comparatively little time will enable you to identify any potential cash flow problems which may arise on a monthly basis. This early identification of potential problems will allow you to take the necessary corrective action and avoid future difficulties.

Chapter 3

Phase 2: Preparation of The Monthly Budget

MONTHLY BUDGET FORMS

Three forms must be prepared to complete Phase 2:

Form MB-1 Annual Fixed Expenses by Month of Payment

Form MB-2 Final Annual Discretionary Expense Summary by Month

Form MB-3 Final Total Budget by Month

ALLOCATION OF ANNUAL FIXED EXPENSES TO MONTH (FORM MB-1)

The information on Form AB-1, Annual Fixed Expenses, is rearranged by month of payment. (Place a paper clip on Form AB-1, page 27 for easy reference.) Start with the first month of the budget projection (in my example, January) and find all January expenses. As each expense is listed, place a mark next to that expense on Form AB-1. This will ensure that all expenses which have been re-entered on Form MB-1 have been recorded only once and will prevent you from recording from "last year's" number column on Form AB-1. The final step should be to add the monthly amounts on Form MB-1 and compare this total with the total on Form AB-1. If the totals do not agree, the work should be rechecked to see that figures were transferred correctly and that last year's figures were not included.

After Form MB-1 is completed, transfer each monthly dollar to Form MB-3, page 71, line 2.

FORM MB-1

ANNUAL FIXED EXPENSES BY MONTH OF PAYMENT

MONTH	EXPENSE CATEGORY	AMOUNT	MONTHLY TOTAL
January	Property Tax	$ 390	
	Dues AAA	$ 35	$ 425*
February	Auto Insurance--Vega	$ 150	$ 150*
March	Auto Insurance--Olds	$ 170	
	CPA License	$ 15	$ 185*
May	Ohio CPA	$ 60	$ 60*
July	Property Tax	$ 390	
	Disability Insurance	$ 210	
	AICPA	$ 40	$ 640*
August	Property Insurance	$ 300	
	Auto Insurance--Vega	$ 150	$ 450*
September	Auto Insurance--Olds	$ 170	$ 170*
October	Life Insurance	$ 275	$ 275*
TOTAL			$2,355
(*Each of the amounts must be transferred to Form MB-3, page 71, line 2.)			

ALLOCATION OF ANNUAL DISCRETIONARY EXPENSES TO MONTH (FORM MB-2)

The completed Forms AB-2 through AB-7--all the adjusted discretionary expenses--will assist in the preparation of Form MB-2. Form MB-2 represents the month in which payment is made, which is usually the month following the purchase or incurrence of the event. While it is difficult to make these estimates, a sincere effort should be made to accurately project the payments. To help you, we will review how I projected my family's expenditure pattern. For easy reference, place paper clips on Forms AB-2 through AB-7.

Form AB-2--Clothes: Most of my clothing purchases are in the spring and fall. I arbitrarily select May and October and put $225 for those two months next to "Harper" on the clothing line. Jane and Sal acquire items more on an ongoing basis except in December and January because of Christmas. Drew's purchases are more random. I approximate how much each will spend for clothing and allocate an amount for each family member, for each month selected.

Form AB-3--Home & Auto: Paint house in June; pay for paint in July ($250); Have Vega tuned in May; pay in June ($50); Have Oldsmobile tuned in June; pay in July ($120). The garage door will be replaced in August, paid in September ($500). Storm windows fitted in April, paid in May ($500).

Form AB-4--Medical: Dental, January and April ($50 each); Jane and Drew's physicals in late July, paid in August ($100); Sal and my physicals are usually in September, paid in October ($250).

Form AB-5--Christmas: Charges begin in September with first payments in October and usually go through February. The amounts selected for each month are arbitrary.

Form AB-6--Vacation: Vacation will be in the later part of June and early July. Cash for June is $300; July is $600; charge payments for August are $100; September is $200. These amounts are approximations.

Form AB-6--Subscriptions: The date of payment for subscriptions can be found on the label and is given as the expiration date.

Form AB-7--Uncertain: I always budget for uncertain events in January ($350) to get it in early.

The final step in Form MB-2 is to add each month's expenses and move to Form MB-3 on page 71.

FORM MB-2

ANNUAL DISCRETIONARY EXPENSE

By Month

EXPENSE CATEGORY	SOURCE	JAN	FEB	MAR	APR	MAY	JUN	JUL	AUG	SEP	OCT	NOV	DEC	TOTAL
Clothes:	AB-2													
Harper	AB-2					225					225			450
Sal	AB-2		75	50	50	25	100	50	25	50	50	25		500
Drew	AB-2		50	50	150		100			100	50			500
Jane	AB-2		100	50	50	100	50	50	50	100	50	50		650
Paint House	AB-3							250						250
Auto	AB-3						50	120						170
Garage Door	AB-3								500					500
Storm Window	AB-3					500								500
Medical	AB-4	50			50				100		250			450
Christmas	AB-5	235	200								100	100	200	835
Subscription	AB-6							9	16			36	28	89
Vacation	AB-6						300	600	100	200				1,200
Uncertain	AB-7	350												350
Annual Discretionary*		635	425	150	300	850	600	1,079	791	450	725	211	228	$6,444

*Transfer totals to MB-3, line 7.

FINAL TOTAL BUDGET BY MONTH (FORM MB-3)

Source of Information

Annual Fixed	Form MB-1,	page 67
Fixed Monthly	Form AB-9,	page 45
Monthly Operational	Form AB-10,	page 60
Monthly Receipts	Form AB-11,	page 49

Computation: $\frac{\$25,527}{\text{months } 12} = \$2,127.75$

Because of rounding, we need $2,130 for last month
Discretionary Expenses Form MB-2, page 69

Some Comments On Form MB-3, the dollar amounts on the line designated "Total Monthly Cash Available for Discretionary Expenses" (line 6) is positive each month, which indicates that the monthly receipts are sufficient to pay for the monthly "necessary expenses": annual fixed, monthly fixed, and monthly operational.

As is the situation here, most budgets will indicate that there are adequate funds for necessary expenses and that the discretionary expenses are where problems may exist. This is extremely important because we have control over discretionary expenses, both how much we spend and when the payment will be made. I am convinced that most budgets will yield these same results--necessary expenses will be covered by monthly receipts. It is a great psychological lift for most people, when they discover they have more control than they realized.

On the bottom line on Form MB-3, we see a $227 deficit for the first month. An examination of my discretionary expense list indicates that the $350 for uncertain events was included in January. With this reminder, I am not particularly worried about January.

I always show a zero balance at the beginning so that my total desired savings (in this case $1,200) will agree with the AB-12 total amount saved. This also provides a much clearer picture of my expenses and receipts for the year.

The only other two months where a cash problem and potential deficit may arise are August ($76) and October ($30). Because most of the months in which the discretionary expenses were to be incurred (Form MB-2) represented an educated guess and because I can control these expenses, I don't re-do the monthly budget nor am I particularly concerned.

If I proceed no further, I now have a very clear picture as to my monthly cash flow and approximately what my monthly cash position should be. I know that I should have some cash available in March, April, May, June, and July. I will need all of this cash for August through October and will not have the $1,200 for permanent investment and disposition until November and December.

If you are interested in trying to manage more closely on a month-to-month basis, you should proceed to Chapter 4 where I use Phase 2's basic form. Completion of Form MB-3 would be an invaluable source of information for those people suddenly alone with the responsibility of managing their finances.

FORM MB-3

FINAL TOTAL BUDGET SUMMARY

	YEAR: ______ MONTH:	JAN	FEB	MAR	APR	MAY	JUN	JUL	AUG	SEP	OCT	NOV	DEC	TOTAL
1	Monthly Receipts (AB-11)	2,127	2,127	2,127	2,127	2,127	2,127	2,127	2,127	2,127	2,127	2,127	2,130	25,527
	Add:													
2	Annual Fixed (MB-1) +	425	150	185	-	60	-	640	450	170	275	-	-	2,355
3	Monthly Fixed (AB-9) +	444	444	444	444	444	444	444	444	444	444	444	444	5,328
4	Monthly Operational (AB-10) +	850	850	850	850	850	850	850	850	850	850	850	850	10,200
5	Total (lines 2, 3, 4)	1,719	1,444	1,479	1,294	1,354	1,294	1,934	1,744	1,464	1,569	1,294	1,294	17,883
	Deduct line 5 from line 1 to get line 6													
6	Cash Available for Discretionary Expenses	408	683	648	833	773	833	193	383	663	558	833	836	7,644
7	Deduct Discretionary Expenses -	635	425	150	300	850	600	1,079	791	450	725	211	228	6,444
8	Total Cash Available After All Expenses This Month													
	Cash Excess		258	498	533		233			213		622	608	
	Cash Short ( )	(227)				(77)		(886)	(408)		(167)			
9	Add Beginning Balance +	-0-	(227)	31	529	1,062	985	1,218	332	(76)	137	(30)	592	
10	Ending Balance +		31	529	1,062	985	1,218	332		137		592	1,200	1,200
	Negative ( )	(227							(76)		(30)			

Chapter 4

Phase 3: Monthly Management

MINI/MAX SAVINGS PROJECTION (FORM MM-1)

I prepare a schedule of what I refer to as "Mini/Max Savings per Projection." For example, let us return to Form MB-3 for the month of January. My annual fixed, monthly fixed, and operational expenses will be spent each month. The only flexibility is in the monthly discretionary amount. If I spend none of the $635 for estimated discretionary expenses, I would be saving $408 (Form M-1, page 75, line 1), and if I spend all of the $635, I would have a negative savings of $227 (schedule MM-1, page 75, line 2). For February, I have a potential maximum savings of $683, and if I add that to the potential maximum for January of $408, I have a potential maximum savings for the two months of $1,091 (Form MM-1, line 3). The Mini/Max Savings Projection can be found on the next page on Form MM-1. This form tells me both the minimum and maximum amounts that I could be placing into temporary savings each month. An additional use for this form is explained under the section entitled "Monthly Receipts/Expenses."

FORM MM-1

MINI/MAX SAVINGS PROJECTION

LINE	JAN	FEB	MAR	APR	MAY	JUN	JUL	AUG	SEP	OCT	NOV	DEC
1. Maximum monthly savings	408	683	648	833	773	833	193	383	663	558	833	836
2. Minimum monthly savings *	(227)	258	498	533	(77)	233	(886)	(408)	213	(167)	622	608
3. Maximum year-to-date savings	408	1091	1739	2572	3345	4178	4371	4754	5417	5975	6808	7644
4. Minimum year-to-date savings	(227)	31	529	1062	985	1218	332	(76)	137	(30)	592	1200

If after deducting monthly expenses from monthly cash receipts you are saving:

1. an amount between the minimum (line 2) and maximum (line 1); and
2. your accumulative savings for the year fall between minimum (line 4) and maximum (line 3),

then you are effectively managing your finances and should be achieving your desired financial goals.

*These amounts are the minimum savings necessary each month in order to pay all projected expenses and save $1,200 for the year.

MONTHLY RECEIPTS/EXPENSES (FORM MM-2)

I prepare Form MM-2 on the first day of each month. I list cash receipts for the month from all sources. Next I total all of my bills and add the allowance amount for monthly operational to obtain total monthly expenses, which are then deducted from total cash receipts. The final amount available for savings for that month should fall somewhere between the mini/max projection for that month.

If the amount available is less than the amount for that month on line 2 of Form MM-1, it is a warning signal that my expenses may be too high and that I should examine actual expenses to determine the reason. It may simply be that I have incurred some of my discretionary expenses earlier than originally anticipated. If my savings are higher than the maximum (line 1, Form MM-1), I may have forgotten to pay an expense or one of my fixed annual expenses may have been deferred. I add the monthly savings to the amount saved previously and compare this total to the mini/max cumulative totals on Form MM-1 (lines 3 and 4). Again if the amount is either too low or high, the variance serves as a warning signal for investigation.

For example, assume that my total receipts for April were $2,127 and I write the following checks:

Rikes	$ 75
Elder Beerman	125
Dayton Power & Light	90
Church	50
State Fidelity	218
Master Charge	40
Dr. Williamson	50
Ohio Bell	35
TOTAL	$683

Using this information, I complete Form MM-2 on the next page. I must compare two dollar amounts to Form MM-1. First, the monthly amount available for savings of $594 should be compared to lines 1 and 2. Then the actual cumulative savings to date of $1,694 is compared with the projected savings--lines 3 and 4. In both cases, the monthly savings and cumulative savings exceed the minimum projected which is an indication that my spending is under control. Note, I did not have to record any actual detailed expenses for the months to gain control.

Other than maintaining envelopes with cash amounts for the first few months of a budget year, my monthly management is relatively easy and simple. If I become concerned about a particular expense, I may attempt to list all of the expenditures to date in that category and compare them to the original budget to determine how much is still available. I did this in the early years with clothing. I often re-examine the budget to determine on an informal basis how much is available and how much has been spent. If you care to make a more formal analysis, Forms MM-3, MM-4, and MM-5 have been provided.

FORM MM-2

MONTHLY RECEIPTS/EXPENSES

MONTH ____________________

Take-Home Pay		$ 2,127
Other Income: ______________________		$ -0-
TOTAL CASH RECEIPTS		$ 2,127
Checks:		
Rikes	$ 75	
Elder Beerman	125	
Dayton Power and Light	90	
Church	50	
State Fidelity (House Payment)	218	
Master Charge	40	
Dr. Williamson	50	
Ohio Bell	35	
TOTAL CHECKS (deduct from Total Cash Receipts)		$ 683
Amount available for operational expenses and savings		$ 1,444
Deduct: Operational Expenses (AB-10, page 60)		$ 850
Amount available for savings and future month's expenses (compare to Mini/Max MM-1, lines 1 and 2)		$ 594
ADD: Amount in Savings (assume)		$ 1,100
SAVINGS TOTAL TO DATE (compare to Mini/Max, lines 3 and 4)		$ 1,694

OPTIONAL FORMS (FORMS MM-3, MM-4, AND MM-5)

To gain very precise information about spending, the following forms may be used:

Form MM-3 allows you to capture the amount spent for each day of the month by expense category. Each expense total by expense category can then be put on Form MM-4 along with the monthly budget to obtain a variance. Form MM-4 also has columns for year-to-date comparisons. Last month's year-to-date amounts are added to this month's amounts. Form MM-5 enables you to capture total costs for one or several expenses by months. You can use this form when a cost may need closer control. The primary tools for monthly management are Forms MM-1 and MM-2, although the others can be useful on occasion.

This budget process has enabled my family to have a good understanding of expenses, and that understanding has provided us real control of our personal finances. It can do the same for you.

FORM MM-3

MONTHLY EXPENSE CONTROL SHEET

DAYS OF THE MONTH

EXPENSE CATEGORY	1	2	3	4	5	6	7	8	9	10	11	12	13	14	15	16

DAYS OF THE MONTH

EXPENSE CATEGORY	17	18	19	20	21	22	23	24	25	26	27	28	29	30	31	

FORM MM-4

MONTHLY PERFORMANCE REPORT

MONTH ____________________

EXPENSE CATEGORY	MONTH			YEAR-TO-DATE		
	BUDGET	ACTUAL	DIFFERENCE	BUDGET	ACTUAL	DIFFERENCE

FORM MM-5

INDIVIDUAL EXPENSE ANALYSIS

MONTH	EXPENSE CATEGORY			
JANUARY				
FEBRUARY				
MARCH				
APRIL				
MAY				
JUNE				
JULY				
AUGUST				
SEPTEMBER				
OCTOBER				
NOVEMBER				
DECEMBER				
TOTAL				

Chapter 5

Budget Forms

FORM AB-1

ANNUAL EXPENSES--FIXED *

EXPENSE	PAYMENT MONTH(S)	LAST YEAR'S COST	THIS YEAR'S COST	NO. OF PAY-MENTS	TOTAL COST THIS YEAR

* Place paper clip on page 27 for easy reference.

FORM AB-2

ANNUAL EXPENSES--DISCRETIONARY *

EXPENSE CATEGORY	LAST YEAR	THIS YEAR	REVISIONS			
			1	2	3	4

* Place paper clip on page 31 for easy reference.

FORM AB-3

ANNUAL EXPENSES--DISCRETIONARY
HOUSEHOLD & AUTO--REPLACEMENT *

LAST YEAR ACTUAL		REVISIONS				
		1	2	3	4	5
THIS YEAR PLANNED						
MAINTAIN:						
CUT COSTS:						
IMPROVE:						

* Place paper clip on page 33 for easy reference.

FORM AB-4

ANNUAL EXPENSES--DISCRETIONARY *

EXPENSE CATEGORY	LAST YEAR	THIS YEAR	REVISIONS			
			1	2	3	4

* Place paper clip on page 35 for easy reference.

FORM AB-5

ANNUAL EXPENSES--DISCRETIONARY *

____

EXPENSE CATEGORY	LAST YEAR	THIS YEAR	REVISIONS			
			1	2	3	4

* Place paper clip on page 37 for easy reference.

FORM AB-6

ANNUAL EXPENSES--DISCRETIONARY *

OTHER

EXPENSE CATEGORY	LAST YEAR	THIS YEAR	REVISIONS			
			1	2	3	4

* Place paper clip on page 39 for easy reference.

FORM AB-7

ANNUAL EXPENSES--DISCRETIONARY *

UNCERTAIN

EXPENSE CATEGORY	LAST YEAR	THIS YEAR	REVISIONS			
			1	2	3	4

* Place paper clip on page 41 for easy reference.

FORM AB-8

PRELIMINARY SUMMARY OF ANNUAL DISCRETIONARY EXPENSES *

EXPENSE CATEGORY	THIS YEAR	REVISIONS			
		1	2	3	4

* Place paper clip on page 43 for easy reference.

FORM AB-9

MONTHLY EXPENSES--FIXED*

EXPENSE CATEGORY	LAST YEAR	THIS YEAR	REVISIONS		
			1	2	3

* Place paper clip on page 45 for easy reference.

FORM AB-10

MONTHLY EXPENSES--OPERATIONAL*

EXPENSE CATEGORY	LAST YEAR	THIS YEAR	REVISIONS		
			1	2	3

* Place paper clip on page 47 for easy reference.

FORM AB-11

COMPUTATION OF CASH RECEIPTS FOR COMING YEAR **

1. Estimate range of annual salary increment and use midpoint to increase.

2. Increase gross wages by average percentage.

   Last Year's Gross Wages:

3. Compute take-home percentage (use last year's payroll check stubs).

   Last Year's Net :

   Last Year's Gross :

4. Multiply take-home percentage (line 3) times estimated gross wages this year (line 2).

   ______________________________ = __________

5. Reduce by any additional anticipated taxes. = __________

6. Add: Any additional sources of income = __________

   and

7. Deduct: Any taxes which will be due = __________

8. Estimated Total Cash Receipt = $__________*

* Transfer amount to AB-12, page 51, line 1.

** Place paper clip on page 49 for easy reference.

FORM AB-12

BUDGET SUMMARY--ANNUAL *

LINE	THIS YEAR	REVISIONS 1	REVISIONS 2
Annual Cash Receipts			
Add:			
Annual Fixed Expenses +			
Monthly Fixed Expenses +			
Monthly Operational Expenses +			
Total (lines 2, 3, 4)			
Deduct: line 5 from line 1 (Annual Cash Receipts) to get line 6			
Cash Available for Discretionary Expenses			
Deduct Discretionary Expenses -			
Total Cash Available After All Expenses			
Cash Excess			
Cash Short ( )			
Deduct Desired Savings			
Required Adjustment			

* Place paper clip on page 51 for easy reference.

FORM MB-1

ANNUAL FIXED EXPENSES BY MONTH OF PAYMENT *

MONTH	EXPENSE CATEGORY	AMOUNT	MONTHLY TOTAL

* Place paper clip on page 67 for easy reference.

FORM MB-2

ANNUAL DISCRETIONARY EXPENSE *

By Month

EXPENSE CATEGORY	SOURCE													TOTAL

* Place paper clip on page 69 for easy reference.

FORM MB-3

FINAL TOTAL BUDGET SUMMARY *

YEAR: ______ MONTH:													TOTAL
Monthly Receipts (AB-11)													
Add: Annual Fixed (MB-1) +													
Monthly Fixed (AB-9) +													
Monthly Operational (AB-10) +													
Total (lines 2, 3, 4)													
Deduct line 5 from line 1 to get line 6													
Cash Available for Discretionary Expenses													
Deduct Discretionary Expenses −													
Total Cash Available After All Expenses This Month													
Cash Excess													
Cash Short ( )													
Add Beginning Balance +													
Ending Balance +													
Negative ( )													

* Place paper clip on page 71 for easy reference.

FORM MB-3

FINAL TOTAL BUDGET SUMMARY *

YEAR: ______ MONTH:													TOTAL
Monthly Receipts (AB-11)													
Add: Annual Fixed (MB-1) + Monthly Fixed (AB-9) + Monthly Operational + (AB-10)													
Total (lines 2, 3, 4)													
Deduct line 5 from line 1 to get line 6 Cash Available for Discretionary Expenses Deduct Discretionary Expenses –													
Total Cash Available After All Expenses This Month Cash Excess Cash Short ( ) Add Beginning Balance +													
Ending Balance + Negative ( )													

* Place paper clip on page 71 for easy reference.

FORM MM-1

MINI/MAX SAVINGS PROJECTION *

LINE												
1. Maximum monthly savings												
2. Minimum monthly savings *												
3. Maximum year-to-date savings												
4. Minimum year-to-date savings												

If after deducting monthly expenses from monthly cash receipts you are saving:

1. an amount between the minimum (line 2) and maximum (line 1); and

2. your accumulative savings for the year fall between minimum (line 4) and maximum (line 3),

then you are effectively managing your finances and should be achieving your desired financial goals.

*Place paper clip on page 75 for easy reference.

**These amounts are the minimum savings necessary each month in order to pay all projected expenses and save $1,200 for the year.

FORM MM-1

MINI/MAX SAVINGS PROJECTION *

LINE												
1. Maximum monthly savings												
2. Minimum monthly savings *												
3. Maximum year-to-date savings												
4. Minimum year-to-date savings												

If after deducting monthly expenses from monthly cash receipts you are saving:

1. an amount between the minimum (line 2) and maximum (line 1); and

2. your accumulative savings for the year fall between minimum (line 4) and maximum (line 3),

then you are effectively managing your finances and should be achieving your desired financial goals.

**These amounts are the minimum savings necessary each month in order to pay all projected expenses and save $1,200 for the year.

*Place paper clip on page 75 for easy reference.

FORM MM-2

MONTHLY RECEIPTS/EXPENSES *

MONTH ____________________

Take-Home Pay		$______
Other Income: ______________________		$______
TOTAL CASH RECEIPTS		$______
Checks:		
______________________	$______	
______________________	______	
______________________	______	
______________________	______	
______________________	______	
______________________	______	
______________________	______	
______________________	______	
______________________	______	
______________________	______	
______________________	______	
TOTAL CHECKS (deduct from Total Cash Receipts)		$______
Amount available for operational expenses and savings		$______
Deduct: Operational Expenses (AB-10, page 47)		$______
Amount available for savings and future month's expenses (compare to Mini/Max MM-1, lines 1 and 2)		$______
ADD: Amount in Savings (assume)		$______
SAVINGS TOTAL TO DATE (compare to Mini/Max, lines 3 and 4)		$______

* Place paper clip on page 77 for easy reference.

FORM MM-2

MONTHLY RECEIPTS/EXPENSES *

MONTH ____________________

Take-Home Pay $ ________

Other Income: ______________________________ $ ________

TOTAL CASH RECEIPTS $ ________

Checks:

______________________________ $ ________

______________________________ ________

______________________________ ________

______________________________ ________

______________________________ ________

______________________________ ________

______________________________ ________

______________________________ ________

______________________________ ________

______________________________ ________

______________________________ ________

TOTAL CHECKS (deduct from Total Cash Receipts) $ ________

Amount available for operational expenses and savings $ ________

Deduct: Operational Expenses (AB-10, page 47) $ ________

Amount available for savings and future month's expenses (compare to Mini/Max MM-1, lines 1 and 2) $ ________

ADD: Amount in Savings (assume) $ ________

SAVINGS TOTAL TO DATE (compare to Mini/Max, lines 3 and 4) $ ________

* Place paper clip on page 77 for easy reference.

FORM MM-2

MONTHLY RECEIPTS/EXPENSES *

MONTH ____________________

Take-Home Pay $ ________

Other Income: ______________________________________ $ ________

TOTAL CASH RECEIPTS $ ________

Checks:

________________________________ $ ________

________________________________ ________

________________________________ ________

________________________________ ________

________________________________ ________

________________________________ ________

________________________________ ________

________________________________ ________

________________________________ ________

________________________________ ________

________________________________ ________

TOTAL CHECKS (deduct from Total Cash Receipts) $ ________

Amount available for operational expenses and savings $ ________

Deduct Operational Expenses (AB-10, page 47) $ ________

Amount available for savings and future month's expenses (compare to Mini/Max MM-1, lines 1 and 2) $ ________

ADD: Amount in Savings (assume) $ ________

SAVINGS TOTAL TO DATE (compare to Mini/Max, lines 3 and 4) $ ________

* Place paper clip on page 77 for easy reference.

FORM MM-2

MONTHLY RECEIPTS/EXPENSES *

MONTH ____________________

Take-Home Pay $________

Other Income: ________________________________ $________

TOTAL CASH RECEIPTS $________

Checks:

__________________________ $______

__________________________ ______

__________________________ ______

__________________________ ______

__________________________ ______

__________________________ ______

__________________________ ______

__________________________ ______

__________________________ ______

__________________________ ______

__________________________ ______

TOTAL CHECKS (deduct from Total Cash Receipts) $________

Amount available for operational expenses and savings $________

Deduct Operational Expenses (AB-10, page 47) $________

Amount available for savings and future month's expenses (compare to Mini/Max MM-1, lines 1 and 2) $________

ADD: Amount in Savings (assume) $________

SAVINGS TOTAL TO DATE (compare to Mini/Max, lines 3 and 4) $________

* Place paper clip on page 77 for easy reference.

FORM MM-2

MONTHLY RECEIPTS/EXPENSES *

MONTH ____________________

Take-Home Pay $ __________

Other Income: ______________________________ $ __________

TOTAL CASH RECEIPTS $ __________

Checks:

______________________________ $ __________
______________________________ __________
______________________________ __________
______________________________ __________
______________________________ __________
______________________________ __________
______________________________ __________
______________________________ __________
______________________________ __________
______________________________ __________
______________________________ __________

TOTAL CHECKS (deduct from Total Cash Receipts) $ __________

Amount available for operational expenses and savings $ __________

Deduct Operational Expenses (AB-10, page 47) $ __________

Amount available for savings and future month's expenses
(compare to Mini/Max MM-1, lines 1 and 2) $ __________

ADD: Amount in Savings (assume) $ __________

SAVINGS TOTAL TO DATE (compare to Mini/Max, lines 3 and 4) $ __________

* Place paper clip on page 77 for easy reference.

FORM MM-2

MONTHLY RECEIPTS/EXPENSES *

MONTH ____________________

Take-Home Pay		$ ________
Other Income: ______________________________		$ ________
TOTAL CASH RECEIPTS		$ ________
Checks:		
______________________________	$ ________	
______________________________	________	
______________________________	________	
______________________________	________	
______________________________	________	
______________________________	________	
______________________________	________	
______________________________	________	
______________________________	________	
______________________________	________	
______________________________	________	
TOTAL CHECKS (deduct from Total Cash Receipts)		$ ________
Amount available for operational expenses and savings		$ ________
Deduct Operational Expenses (AB-10, page 47)		$ ________
Amount available for savings and future month's expenses (compare to Mini/Max MM-1, lines 1 and 2)		$ ________
ADD: Amount in Savings (assume)		$ ________
SAVINGS TOTAL TO DATE (compare to Mini/Max, lines 3 and 4)		$ ________

* Place paper clip on page 77 for easy reference.

FORM MM-2

MONTHLY RECEIPTS/EXPENSES *

MONTH ____________________

Take-Home Pay		$ ______
Other Income: ____________________		$ ______
TOTAL CASH RECEIPTS		$ ______
Checks:		
____________________	$ ______	
____________________	______	
____________________	______	
____________________	______	
____________________	______	
____________________	______	
____________________	______	
____________________	______	
____________________	______	
____________________	______	
____________________	______	
TOTAL CHECKS (deduct from Total Cash Receipts)		$ ______
Amount available for operational expenses and savings		$ ______
Deduct Operational Expenses (AB-10, page 47)		$ ______
Amount available for savings and future month's expenses (compare to Mini/Max MM-1, lines 1 and 2)		$ ______
ADD: Amount in Savings (assume)		$ ______
SAVINGS TOTAL TO DATE (compare to Mini/Max, lines 3 and 4)		$ ______

* Place paper clip on page 77 for easy reference.

FORM MM-2

MONTHLY RECEIPTS/EXPENSES *

MONTH ____________________

Take-Home Pay		$ ______
Other Income: ______________________		$ ______
TOTAL CASH RECEIPTS		$ ______
Checks:		
______________________	$ ______	
______________________	______	
______________________	______	
______________________	______	
______________________	______	
______________________	______	
______________________	______	
______________________	______	
______________________	______	
______________________	______	
______________________	______	
TOTAL CHECKS (deduct from Total Cash Receipts)		$ ______
Amount available for operational expenses and savings		$ ______
Deduct Operational Expenses (AB-10, page 47)		$ ______
Amount available for savings and future month's expenses (compare to Mini/Max MM-1, lines 1 and 2)		$ ______
ADD: Amount in Savings (assume)		$ ______
SAVINGS TOTAL TO DATE (compare to Mini/Max, lines 3 and 4)		$ ______

* Place paper clip on page 77 for easy reference.

FORM MM-2

MONTHLY RECEIPTS/EXPENSES *

MONTH ____________________

Take-Home Pay $__________

Other Income: ______________________________ $__________

TOTAL CASH RECEIPTS $__________

Checks:

______________________________ $________

______________________________ ________

______________________________ ________

______________________________ ________

______________________________ ________

______________________________ ________

______________________________ ________

______________________________ ________

______________________________ ________

______________________________ ________

______________________________ ________

TOTAL CHECKS (deduct from Total Cash Receipts) $__________

Amount available for operational expenses and savings $__________

Deduct Operational Expenses (AB-10, page 47) $__________

Amount available for savings and future month's expenses
(compare to Mini/Max MM-1, lines 1 and 2) $__________

ADD: Amount in Savings (assume) $__________

SAVINGS TOTAL TO DATE (compare to Mini/Max, lines 3 and 4) $__________

* Place paper clip on page 77 for easy reference.

FORM MM-2

MONTHLY RECEIPTS/EXPENSES *

MONTH ____________________

Take-Home Pay		$ ________
Other Income: ______________________		$ ________
TOTAL CASH RECEIPTS		$ ________
Checks:		
______________________	$ ________	
______________________	________	
______________________	________	
______________________	________	
______________________	________	
______________________	________	
______________________	________	
______________________	________	
______________________	________	
______________________	________	
______________________	________	
TOTAL CHECKS (deduct from Total Cash Receipts)		$ ________
Amount available for operational expenses and savings		$ ________
Deduct Operational Expenses (AB-10, page 47)		$ ________
Amount available for savings and future month's expenses (compare to Mini/Max MM-1, lines 1 and 2)		$ ________
ADD: Amount in Savings (assume)		$ ________
SAVINGS TOTAL TO DATE (compare to Mini/Max, lines 3 and 4)		$ ________

* Place paper clip on page 77 for easy reference.

FORM MM-2

MONTHLY RECEIPTS/EXPENSES *

MONTH ____________________

Take-Home Pay		$ ________
Other Income: ______________________________		$ ________
TOTAL CASH RECEIPTS		$ ________
Checks:		
______________________________	$ ________	
______________________________	________	
______________________________	________	
______________________________	________	
______________________________	________	
______________________________	________	
______________________________	________	
______________________________	________	
______________________________	________	
______________________________	________	
______________________________	________	
TOTAL CHECKS (deduct from Total Cash Receipts)		$ ________
Amount available for operational expenses and savings		$ ________
Deduct Operational Expenses (AB-10, page 47)		$ ________
Amount available for savings and future month's expenses (compare to Mini/Max MM-1, lines 1 and 2)		$ ________
ADD: Amount in Savings (assume)		$ ________
SAVINGS TOTAL TO DATE (compare to Mini/Max, lines 3 and 4)		$ ________

* Place paper clip on page 77 for easy reference.

FORM MM-2

MONTHLY RECEIPTS/EXPENSES *

MONTH ____________________

Take-Home Pay		$______
Other Income: ______________________		$______
TOTAL CASH RECEIPTS		$______
Checks:		
______________________	$______	
______________________	______	
______________________	______	
______________________	______	
______________________	______	
______________________	______	
______________________	______	
______________________	______	
______________________	______	
______________________	______	
______________________	______	
TOTAL CHECKS (deduct from Total Cash Receipts)		$______
Amount available for operational expenses and savings		$______
Deduct Operational Expenses (AB-10, page 47)		$______
Amount available for savings and future month's expenses (compare to Mini/Max MM-1, lines 1 and 2)		$______
ADD: Amount in Savings (assume)		$______
SAVINGS TOTAL TO DATE (compare to Mini/Max, lines 3 and 4)		$______

* Place paper clip on page 77 for easy reference.

FORM MM-3

MONTHLY EXPENSE CONTROL SHEET

DAYS OF THE MONTH

EXPENSE CATEGORY	1	2	3	4	5	6	7	8	9	10	11	12	13	14	15	16

DAYS OF THE MONTH

EXPENSE CATEGORY	17	18	19	20	21	22	23	24	25	26	27	28	29	30	31	

FORM MM-3

MONTHLY EXPENSE CONTROL SHEET

DAYS OF THE MONTH

EXPENSE CATEGORY	1	2	3	4	5	6	7	8	9	10	11	12	13	14	15	16

DAYS OF THE MONTH

EXPENSE CATEGORY	17	18	19	20	21	22	23	24	25	26	27	28	29	30	31	

FORM MM-3

MONTHLY EXPENSE CONTROL SHEET

DAYS OF THE MONTH

EXPENSE CATEGORY	1	2	3	4	5	6	7	8	9	10	11	12	13	14	15	16

DAYS OF THE MONTH

EXPENSE CATEGORY	17	18	19	20	21	22	23	24	25	26	27	28	29	30	31	

FORM MM-3

MONTHLY EXPENSE CONTROL SHEET

DAYS OF THE MONTH

EXPENSE CATEGORY	1	2	3	4	5	6	7	8	9	10	11	12	13	14	15	16

DAYS OF THE MONTH

EXPENSE CATEGORY	17	18	19	20	21	22	23	24	25	26	27	28	29	30	31	

FORM MM-3

MONTHLY EXPENSE CONTROL SHEET

DAYS OF THE MONTH

EXPENSE CATEGORY	1	2	3	4	5	6	7	8	9	10	11	12	13	14	15	16

DAYS OF THE MONTH

EXPENSE CATEGORY	17	18	19	20	21	22	23	24	25	26	27	28	29	30	31	

FORM MM-3

MONTHLY EXPENSE CONTROL SHEET

DAYS OF THE MONTH

EXPENSE CATEGORY	1	2	3	4	5	6	7	8	9	10	11	12	13	14	15	16

DAYS OF THE MONTH

EXPENSE CATEGORY	17	18	19	20	21	22	23	24	25	26	27	28	29	30	31	

FORM MM-4

MONTHLY PERFORMANCE REPORT

MONTH ____________________

EXPENSE CATEGORY	MONTH			YEAR-TO-DATE		
	BUDGET	ACTUAL	DIFFERENCE	BUDGET	ACTUAL	DIFFERENCE

FORM MM-4

MONTHLY PERFORMANCE REPORT

MONTH ____________________

EXPENSE CATEGORY	MONTH			YEAR-TO-DATE		
	BUDGET	ACTUAL	DIFFERENCE	BUDGET	ACTUAL	DIFFERENCE

FORM MM-4

MONTHLY PERFORMANCE REPORT

MONTH ____________________

EXPENSE CATEGORY	MONTH			YEAR-TO-DATE		
	BUDGET	ACTUAL	DIFFERENCE	BUDGET	ACTUAL	DIFFERENCE

FORM MM-4

MONTHLY PERFORMANCE REPORT

MONTH ______________________

EXPENSE CATEGORY	MONTH			YEAR-TO-DATE		
	BUDGET	ACTUAL	DIFFERENCE	BUDGET	ACTUAL	DIFFERENCE

FORM MM-4

MONTHLY PERFORMANCE REPORT

MONTH ____________________

EXPENSE CATEGORY	MONTH			YEAR-TO-DATE		
	BUDGET	ACTUAL	DIFFERENCE	BUDGET	ACTUAL	DIFFERENCE

FORM MM-5

INDIVIDUAL EXPENSE ANALYSIS

MONTH	EXPENSE CATEGORY			
JANUARY				
FEBRUARY				
MARCH				
APRIL				
MAY				
JUNE				
JULY				
AUGUST				
SEPTEMBER				
OCTOBER				
NOVEMBER				
DECEMBER				
TOTAL				

FORM MM-5

INDIVIDUAL EXPENSE ANALYSIS

MONTH	EXPENSE CATEGORY			
JANUARY				
FEBRUARY				
MARCH				
APRIL				
MAY				
JUNE				
JULY				
AUGUST				
SEPTEMBER				
OCTOBER				
NOVEMBER				
DECEMBER				
TOTAL				

FORM MM-5

INDIVIDUAL EXPENSE ANALYSIS

MONTH	EXPENSE CATEGORY			
JANUARY				
FEBRUARY				
MARCH				
APRIL				
MAY				
JUNE				
JULY				
AUGUST				
SEPTEMBER				
OCTOBER				
NOVEMBER				
DECEMBER				
TOTAL				

INDEX

The Next Step Beyond

SPENDING LESS AND ENJOYING IT MORE

Using Your Personal Computer to Manage Your Money

Now that you understand the concepts behind an effective way of managing your income, you may want to take advantage of the power in your personal computer to make the task that much simpler. The basic worksheets and calculations used in this book are available as software for a variety of popular personal computers.

COMPUTER SYSTEM:

O Atari _______ (Model)   O Apple ______ (Model)   O IBM ______ (Model)   O Coleco ADAM

O Commodore 64   O Other ______________ Please Specify

NAME______________________________________

ADDRESS___________________________________

CITY_________________________STATE________ZIP______

PHONE (   )_______________________________

O CHECK   O MASTER CHARGE   O VISA

__________________ Card Number   __________ Exp Date

______________________________ Signature

Complete the above order form and send to Culverin Corporation, P.O. Box 503, Centerville, Ohio, 45459. The price is $41.00. Ohio residents add 6% sales tax.